PASSWORD
ENGLISH

Textbook 5

ACTIVITIES FOR GROUP WORK

GINN

Contents

WORD LEVEL

Spelling
Spelling strategies	3	14-17
Plural nouns	6	18-19
Prefixes and suffixes	7	20-25
Spelling rules	10	26-27
Transforming words	11	40-41

Vocabulary
Synonyms	13	42-43
Common expressions	14	46-47
Adverbs	16	48-49
Special words	17	54-55
Antonyms	18	56-57
Dictionaries	19	58-63

SENTENCE LEVEL

Grammar
Standard English	22	64-71
Verbs	28	72-77
Grammar strategies	31	80-83
Direct and reported speech	35	86-87
Spoken and written language	36	90-91
Sentence structure	38	94-99
Prepositions	42	100-101

Punctuation
Punctuation revision	44	102-103
Dialogue	45	104-107

TEXT LEVEL

Fiction
Authors	47	110-113
Playscripts	50	116-119
Characters	52	120-125
Structure	55	126-131
Reading strategies	59	132-133
Traditional stories	61	138-143
Point of view	67	144-149
Genres	70	150-153
Cultures and traditions	74	154-157

Poetry
Forms of poetry	78	160-161
Classic poetry	80	166-169

Non-fiction
Recounted texts	82	178-183
Instructions	87	184-189
Explanatory texts	89	190-191
Reports	90	196-197
Persuasive writing	92	204-205
Letters	93	208-213

How to use this book

- read or look carefully
- write
- share or discuss

Notebooks appear on some pages with examples or ideas for your answers!

Spelling strategies

Linking spelling to meaning

> One of the most helpful spelling rules in English is: similar meaning, similar spelling. It works almost all the time!

1. Write these pairs of words from the same family.

magic	soft	muscle	wide	cone
magician	soften	muscular	width	conical

   - Say each word out loud.
   - How does the rule work with these words?

2. Circle the letter in each pair of words that changes its sound.

3. Write one word that belongs to the same family as each of these words.

globe	real	medical	nature	critic
shade	vision	please	final	prime
part	press	produce	nation	know

4. Use a dictionary to help you find more words in each family, and to check their meanings.
   - How does the rule work in these word families?
   - Circle the letter or letters that change their sound.

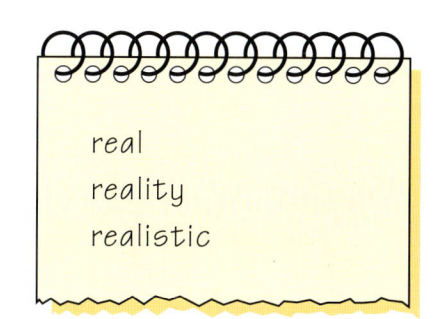

   real
   reality
   realistic

3

Spelling strategies

Building words with prefixes and suffixes

1. A web diagram shows how a root word can be made into longer words by adding prefixes and suffixes.

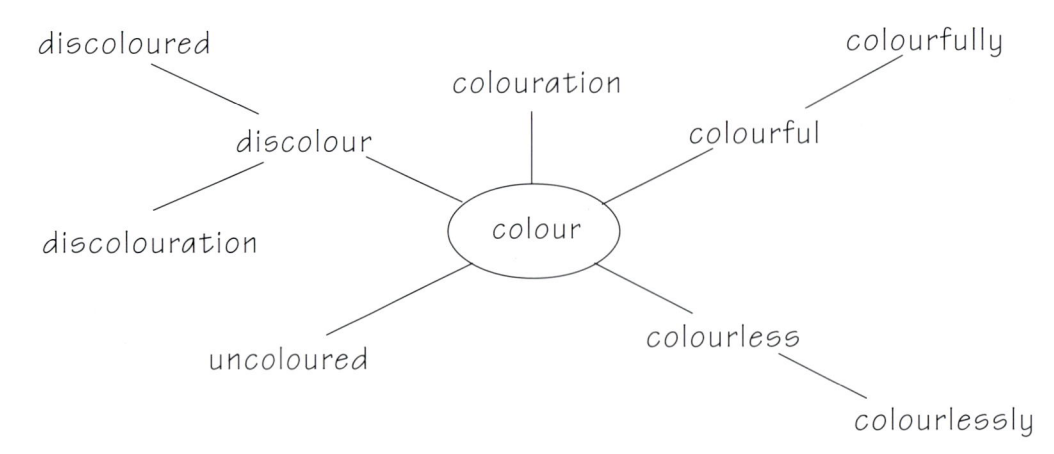

```
discoloured                              colourfully
        colouration
   discolour              colourful
discolouration      colour
        uncoloured       colourless
                                  colourlessly
```

2. Choose five words from the box below. Draw web diagrams to show words that can be built up from each word.

assure	friend	image	appear
favour	courage	direct	able
person	present	forget	compose
grace	nation	manage	organise
place	real	science	act

REMEMBER: sometimes the spelling of the root word is changed when a suffix beginning with a vowel is added.

3. Share and compare your diagrams.

Spelling strategies

Checking spellings

1. There are 14 deliberate spelling mistakes in this poem. A spell-checker would miss them all!

Spellbound
I have a spelling chequer
It came with my PC
It plainly marks four my revue
Miss takes I cannot sea.
I've run this poem threw it
I'm shore your pleased too no;
It's letter perfect in it's weigh
My chequer tolled me sew.

Norman Vandal

2. Find all the mistakes, and write them in a list. Then write the correct version of each word.

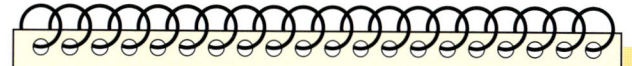

Use a dictionary for help with this.

3. Why did the spell-checker miss them? Write a reason for each word.

4. Write a sentence with some mistakes that a spell-checker would miss.
   - If you can, use a computer for this.
   - What happens with the spell-checker?

Plural nouns

Investigating rules for making plurals

1. Look at this list of nouns.
   Each of them follows a different pattern for pluralisation.

   sheep
   trousers
   monkey
   leaf
   mathematics
   dress
   fairy
   volcano

2. For each word:
   - Write the plural form.
   - Explain the spelling pattern it follows.
   - Write a list of other words that follow the same pattern. Use a dictionary to check.

   sheep
   sheep has no plural form
   other words: fish, buffalo

Prefixes and suffixes

Investigating prefixes of number

1. Many English words are based on Greek and Latin number words. Here are some examples.

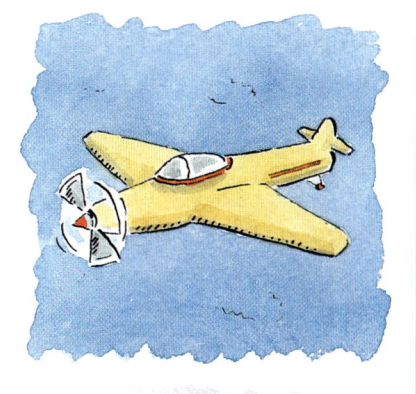

1	unicycle monoplane
2	duet bicycle
3	tricycle
4	quadruped
8	octopus
100	century

2. Write the meaning of each of these words.

3. List at least one other number word beginning with each prefix, and explain each meaning.

4. Use reference books to find the prefixes for 5, 6, 7, 9, 10 and 1000.
   - Write a list of words beginning with each prefix.
   - Explain the meaning of each word.

5. Work out the answer to this puzzle.

Why does the word **October** begin with the prefix for eight?

7

Prefixes and suffixes

Adding suffixes to make adjectives

1. Write these sentences, turning the nouns in brackets into adjectives. You can do this by adding a suffix.

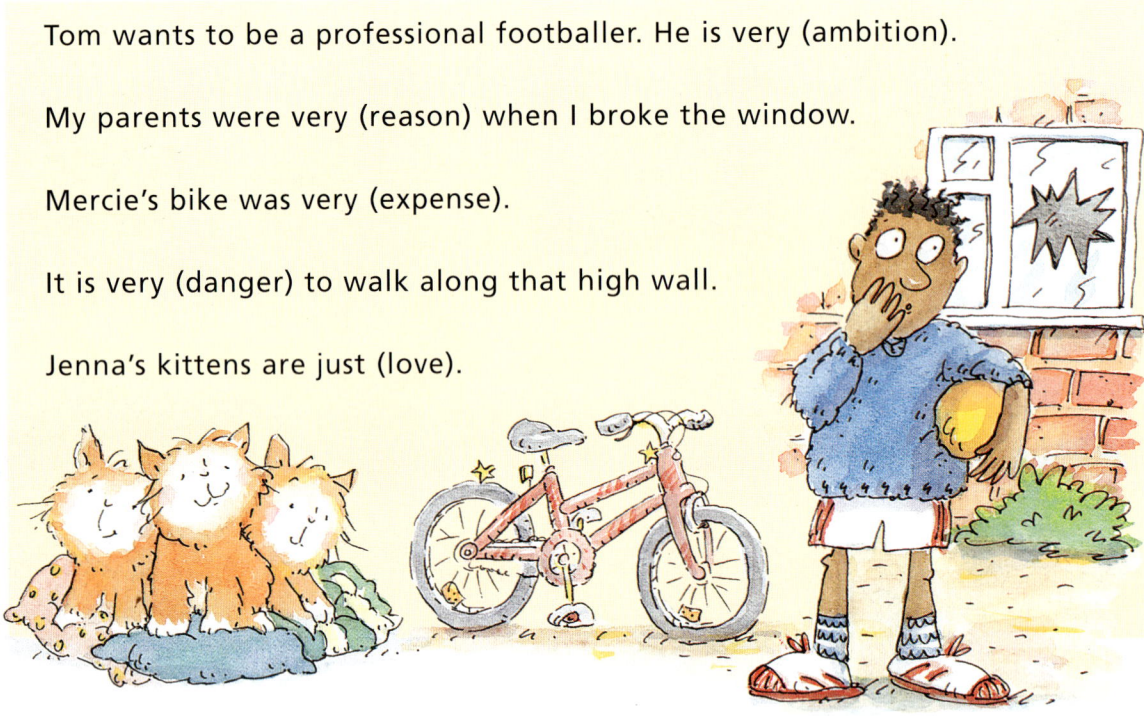

Tom wants to be a professional footballer. He is very (ambition).

My parents were very (reason) when I broke the window.

Mercie's bike was very (expense).

It is very (danger) to walk along that high wall.

Jenna's kittens are just (love).

2. Many adjectives end in the suffixes -ous, -able, and -ive. Write at least two adjectives that use each suffix.

3. Add suffixes to change the verbs in brackets into nouns, so that they fit into each sentence.

My teacher says there has been a big (improve) in my writing.

(Pollute) in the river is getting worse.

The police (investigate) took a long time.

He was badly hurt in a (collide).

The (disappear) of the jewels was discovered last night.

4. Many nouns end in the suffixes -ment, -tion, -sion, and -ance. Write at least two nouns that use each suffix.

Prefixes and suffixes

Using prefixes to form negative words

1. Make the words below negative by adding one of these prefixes.

| in- | dis- | un- | ir- | il- | im- | mis- |

usual	agree	advantage	efficient
entangle	resistible	respect	legal
identified	pure	proper	mortal
wrap	trust	necessary	regular
reversible	use	cover	lead
personal	logical	legible	polite
direct	patient	equal	practical
mature	able	replaceable	understand
fortune	edible	behave	tangle
treat	sane	adventure	secure

2. You can add more than one negative prefix to some of these words.
   - Which ones are they? Write them.
   - Do these words mean just the same?

3. A puzzle: what do these words mean? What is unusual about all of them?

| indignant | inane | disgruntled |
| unkempt | uncouth | inept |

9

Spelling rules

Revising spelling rules

1. Look at these lists of words. Each list shows a certain spelling rule.

   A *hopping, canning, tapping, pinning*

   B *hoping, caning, taping, pining*

   C *heading, beating, walking, jumping*

   D *cheerful, hopeful, successful, resentful*

   E *receive, ceiling, deceive, receipt*

2. Discuss each list of words with your group.
   - Which spelling rule is shown by each list of words?
   - Write notes about your ideas.
   - Choose two more words to fit in each group.

   Use a dictionary for help if you need to!

3. Use one word from each list in a sentence, to show you understand its meaning.

4. Choose a spelling rule not mentioned on this page, and write your own list of words for it.

Transforming words

Changing verbs and nouns

1. Read this passage from Gerald Durrell's book *My Family and Other Animals*.

Scorpions in a Matchbox

Then one day I found a fat female scorpion in the wall, wearing what at first glance appeared to be a pale fawn fur coat. Closer inspection proved that this strange garment was made up of a mass of tiny babies clinging to the mother's back. I was enraptured by this family, and I made up my mind to smuggle them into the house in a matchbox so that I might keep them and watch them grow up. I placed the matchbox carefully on the mantelpiece in the drawing-room and joined the family. Dawdling over my food, feeding Roger under the table and listening to the family arguing, I completely forgot about my exciting new captures. At last Larry, having finished, fetched the cigarettes from the drawing-room, and lying back in his chair he put one in his mouth and picked up the matchbox he had brought.

Now I maintain to this day that the female scorpion meant no harm. She was agitated and a trifle annoyed at being shut up in a matchbox for so long, and so she seized the first opportunity to escape. She hoisted herself out of the box, her babies clinging on desperately, and scuttled on to the back of Larry's hand. There, she paused, her sting curved up at the ready. Larry, feeling the movement of her claws, glanced down to see what it was, and from that moment things got increasingly confused.

Gerald Durrell
My Family and Other Animals

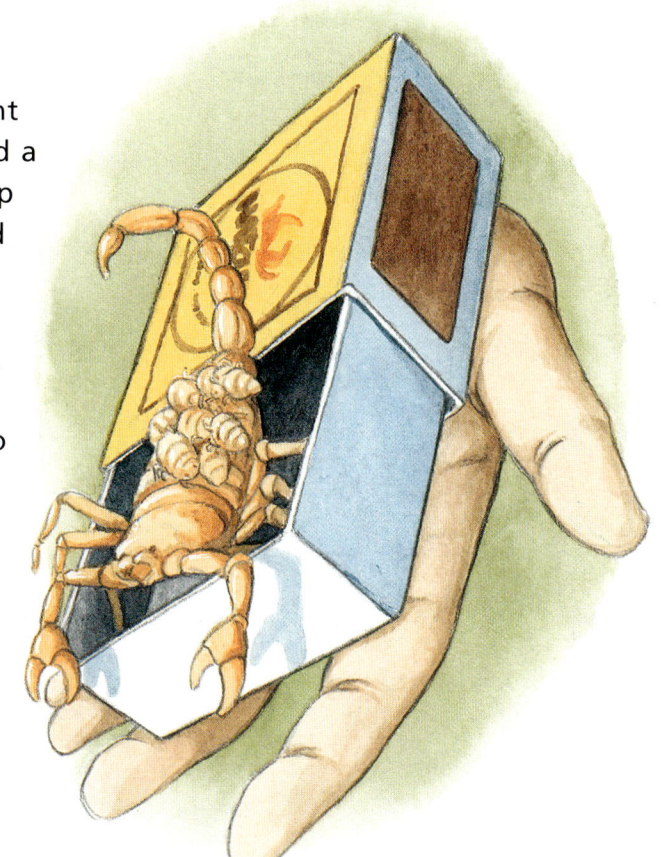

2. These are some of the verbs from the text. Use a dictionary to help you make nouns from these verbs.

(to) appear   (to) grow
(to) argue   (to) maintain
(to) agitate   (to) annoy
(to) seize   (to) confuse

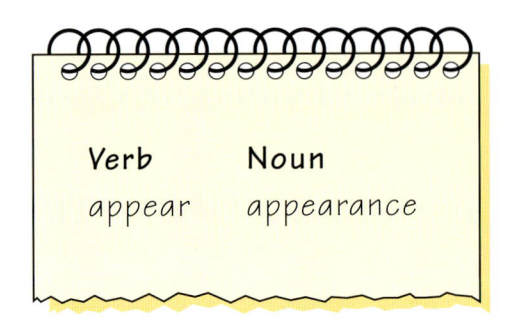

Verb	Noun
appear	appearance

3. Write an alphabetical list of the suffixes used in your answer to the last question.

4. These nouns are used in the text.
   - Which verbs can you make from these nouns?

   inspection   movement   food

   - Use each verb you make in a sentence, to show you understand its meaning.

5. Add -ing and -ed to these verbs. Take care with the spelling!

appear   fetch   pause
watch   seize   confuse
place   escape
call   scuttle

Synonyms

Identifying and using synonyms

1. Read this poem and look for the synonyms.

   The Big Match

   It was such a big, big match –
   But with no trainers for the game,
   It would have been such a pity
   To have missed out – what a shame!

   So I ran off to the High Street –
   Straight down that busy road,
   There was a great big shop display
   With many trainers there on show!

   Inside, I made a purchase –
   The best trainers I could buy,
   "Now I can play the game!" I said
   "Good luck!" the shopkeeper cried!

   Back to the football pitch I rushed –
   Through the crowds I pushed and hurried,
   But then I found, to my concern
   Without me they had won – no worry!

   Anon.

2. Write a list of the eight synonym pairs in this poem.

   street – road – avenue

3. Write one more synonym for each pair.

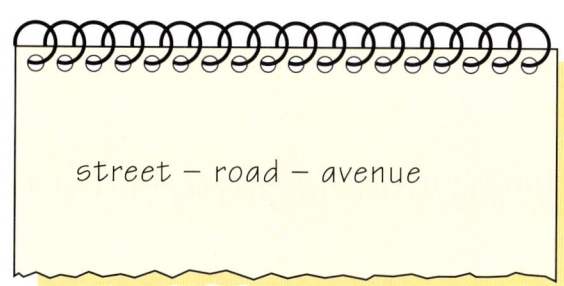

4. Discuss and write notes on the different meanings of the words in each set of synonyms.

5. Now work with your group to write a new verse for the poem.
   - What will happen to the player and the team?
   - What synonyms could you use? Brainstorm a list.
   - Remember to follow the pattern of the other verses!

Common expressions

Exploring expressions

1. Read this poem by Pie Corbett.

An Odd Kettle of Fish

The detectives said that
the books had been cooked.
(They tasted good.)

My teacher said we could
have a free hand.
(I added it to my collection.)

Some people bottle up
their feelings.
(I keep mine in a jar.)

My mother said -
"Hold your tongue!"
(It was too slippery.)

When my sister laughs
she drives me round the bend.
(I catch the bus back.)

Dad told me
to keep a stiff upper lip.
(It's in a box by my bed.)

My uncle is a terrible
name dropper.
(I help my aunt
to sweep them up.)

In the school races
I licked everyone in the class
(It made my tongue sore.)

2. Write the common expression used in each of these verses. Explain what each one means and when people might use it.

3. Think of some more common expressions, and use them to write more verses like the ones in this poem.

14

Common expressions

Explaining expressions

1. Here are some more common expressions.

It goes in one ear and out the other.

It was just a slip of the tongue.

That rings a bell.

It's no good sweeping it under the carpet.

He's bitten off more than he can chew.

She hasn't got a leg to stand on.

He's getting too big for his boots.

We're all in the same boat.

He gets right up my nose.

2. Write an explanation of what each expression means.

3. Choose the three expressions that you like best.
   Write a short conversation for each that shows when they might be used.

15

Adverbs

Using adverbs in context

1. Read this story.

He called _____ into the darkness. He felt like something or someone was whispering _____ into his ear. But every time he stopped to listen, there was no-one there. It's all imagination, he told himself _____ .

He called again, more _____ this time. He was sure he heard something reply to him. A kind of snuffle came _____ out of the darkness. He called out _____ again, but the sound was gone.

Just around the next corner came his chance. He jumped into the doorway, screaming _____ until he saw him. It was Prince, his dog, barking _____ . He gave Prince a hug, but gasped _____ when he saw a note tied around his collar. What did it say?

2. Write out the text, using suitable adverbs in the spaces.

3. Now write a second version of the text.
   - Use a new set of adverbs in the spaces.
   - Try to make the story completely different!

> He called loudly into the darkness.

Special words

Exploring dialects

1. Sally is from Scotland and has gone to Florida to visit Amy, her American penfriend. Read this conversation between them.

Panel 1:
- Amy: Hey, look Sal! My mom's given me a whole load of cookies to take to the park!
- Sally: Och, I'm no' sure I wannae eat anything, ye ken?

Panel 2:
- Amy: Gee, that sucks, Sal! Mom spent all morning making cookies and candy for us!
- Sally: Well, why don't we share them with the wee bonnie bairns from next door?

Panel 3:
- Sally: I'll come with ye!
- Amy: Great – we can play ball with them, too! I'll get the gear from the trunk of the car!

Panel 4:
- Amy: Hey, guys – here are the catching mitts!
- Sally: Be careful you don't throw anything in tae the windows!

2. Write a list of all the dialect words that Sally and Amy use.

   REMEMBER: dialect words are non-standard forms of English.

   mom = mother

3. Now rewrite their conversation in standard English.

4. Share your version of the conversation with the rest of your group.
   - Which do you think sounds better?
   - Give reasons for your answer.

17

Antonyms

Adding antonyms to sentences

1. Read each of these sentences.

   The holiday <u>began</u> with a long car drive.

   They travelled all <u>day</u> without stopping.

   At <u>midnight</u> they finally stopped.

   In the distance, they could just see a steep <u>hill</u>.

   The road was <u>narrow</u> with trees on both sides.

   The traffic was <u>heavy</u> and showed no sign of slowing down.

   When they got to their holiday house the sea was <u>calm</u>.

   The next day the beach was very <u>crowded</u>.

   Out to sea, the fishing fleet was heading <u>south</u>.

   The sky was as blue as Jane could remember: it <u>always</u> rained on family holidays.

2. Which antonyms could be used to replace the underlined words?
   - Discuss the ideas with your group.
   - Brainstorm a list of possible words.

3. Write each sentence, using the antonyms you have discussed.

4. Now write three more sentences, using a word and its opposite in each one.

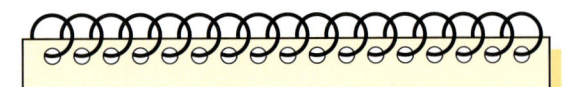

   As I went <u>up</u> the stairs, my dad came <u>down</u>.

Dictionaries

Investigating shortened forms

1. The underlined words in these sentences are all in their shortened form.

   Our class has just got a new computer with <u>32MB</u> of <u>RAM</u>. It is linked up to the <u>phone</u> line so that we can use it to send and receive <u>e-mail</u> messages.

   Our teacher saw an <u>ad</u> for it in a computer <u>mag</u>.

   There's a great new adventure game where you are a pilot and have to use <u>radar</u> and <u>lasers</u>.

   There's a good football game too, with a <u>ref</u> that blows a whistle when there is a foul, and you can choose the <u>goalie's</u> kit.

   On the music <u>CD-ROM</u> you can watch extracts from <u>pop videos</u>. It has wonderful <u>hi-fi stereo</u> sound.

   If you plug in the <u>mike</u>, you can record yourself singing!

2. How have the words in the text been shortened?
   - Make a table with three columns.
   - Write the full form of each of the words in the correct column.
   - You will need a dictionary.

short form	full word	omitted letters
MB	megabytes	-ega -ytes

3. Think of some more shortened forms for this table.
   Write the full form of the word beside it.

19

Dictionaries

Explaining synonyms

1. Imagine that you are working on a dictionary of synonyms. The editor has given you these four sets of words with a similar meaning.

dirty *(adj)* filthy, grimy, dusty, greasy, grubby, muddy, polluted, contaminated, foul

old *(adj)* ancient, early, historic, prehistoric, elderly, aged, grown-up, antique, worn-out, used

change *(v)* alter, revise, adjust, vary, adapt, swap, exchange, transform, switch, replace

cut *(v)* carve, chop, clip, gash, mow, shear, slice, slit, hack, snip, trim

2. Write the dictionary entry for two words from each set. Explain the meaning of each word and give an example of how you would use the word.
   - Look at the Big Book page for ideas about how to set this out.
   - Start by explaining what the words have in common.
   - Then explain the differences in meaning and use.

If some of the words in a set are very close in meaning and use, try grouping and explaining them together.

3. Which words are most difficult to explain? Why?

Dictionaries

Compiling a personal dictionary

1. Write entries for a dictionary of words that are special or important for you and your friends.

   You could include words to do with:

   your school and neighbourhood
   games you play
   food and drink
   hobbies
   clothes
   computers
   music
   sport

2. Write an entry for each word on a separate sheet of paper. Explain:
   - what it means
   - how and when it is used
   - how to pronounce it, if this is difficult or unusual.

   If you can, give information about the word's origins as well.

3. As your group's collection of special words grows, share them with other groups working on this.
   - Sort all the words into alphabetical order.
   - Make your own class dictionary!

Standard English

Revising parts of speech

1. Read the beginning of this traditional story from Ireland.

The Sad Story of the Children of Lir

Long ago, there lived in Ireland a girl named Fionnuala. She had a father and three brothers, but no mother, for her mother had died when her youngest brother was born. Of course, Fionnuala missed her mother very much, but she loved her father and her three brothers. Since they loved her equally, she had quite a happy life.

Then one day her father, whose name was Lir, told her that he was going to marry again.

"I am lonely without your mother," he said, "so I am going to marry her younger sister, your Aunt Aoife."

Of course, Fionnuala and her brothers already knew their Aunt Aoife. Aoife had always been friendly and Fionnuala thought it might be nice to have another woman in the house amongst all those men.

The trouble was that Aoife changed when she became their step-mother. She became jealous of Fionnuala and her brothers Aodh, Fiachra and Conn, because they were such beautiful and clever children and their father was so proud of them. When Lir was there she would pretend to be fond of them too but, when his back was turned, she would sometimes be unkind to them.

2. Read the second sentence again.
   - Which word is a pronoun?
   - What name could be used instead of this pronoun?

3. In the last sentence of the first paragraph, how many people does *they* refer to?

4. The sentence of speech in the third paragraph could be written as indirect speech. Fill in the missing pronouns.

He said that _____ was lonely without _____ and so _____ was going to marry her younger sister, Aoife.

5. Use a pronoun to replace each set of underlined words:

Of course, Fionnuala and her brothers already knew their Aunt Aoife.

6. Join these sentences together.
   - Their father married Aoife. Aoife was their mother's sister.
   - The children were quite happy at the news. Their father had told them the news.
   - Fionnuala missed her mother. Her mother was dead.
   - Lir had four children. Lir loved them very much.

7. Make up four questions of your own about this story.
   Each question should include a pronoun.
   Try them out with your group to test their knowledge of the story!

Standard English

Revising agreement

1. Read this poem about a tree.

The Tree in the Garden

There's a tree out in our garden which is very nice to climb,
And I often go and climb it when it's fine in the summer time.
And when I've climbed right up it I pretend it's not a tree
But a ship in which I'm sailing, far away across the sea.

Its branches are the rigging and the grass so far below
I make believe's the ocean over which my ship must go;
And when the wind is blowing then I really seem to be
A-sailing, sailing, sailing, far away across the sea.

Then I hunt for desert islands and I very often find
A chest stuffed full of treasure which some pirate's left behind...
My good ship's hold is filled with gold – it all belongs to me
For I've found it when I'm sailing far away across the sea.

It's a lovely game to play at – though the tree trunk's rather green,
Still, when I'm in my bath at night I always come quite clean.
And so through all the summer, in my good ship Treasure-Tree,
I shall often go a-sailing far away across the sea.

Christine Chandler

2. Rewrite the poem entirely in the plural. Make sure all the nouns, pronouns and verbs agree!

3. When you have finished, compare your version with the others in your group.

4. Discuss whether you prefer the poem in the singular or in the plural. Why?

> There **are trees** out in our **gardens** which **are** very nice to climb.

Standard English

Changing tenses and subjects

1. Read this text about a woman with a Cockney accent.

Talking Cockney

You could say I had a slightly Cockney accent, when talking with friends, that is. When I'm talking to my friends, I can be myself. I don't have to impress anyone, like a new boss for example. I interrupt them, we have arguments, but it's me, my real voice. If I suddenly changed to a rather posher accent, my friends would either think I was just pretending or that I was 'becoming above myself'.

It's different when I'm with my mum, though. When I'm talking to her, I remember not to drop so many Hs or use slang as my mum says it sounds terrible. I try to be more respectful in the way I speak to my mum as she's always telling me to speak properly, but what does she mean by this? She comes from Ireland and the way she speaks is far from perfect, but she doesn't understand that my voice is typical of where I live.

Accents and voices of all kinds make up the English language, so who can say one of them is bad? Americans talk how they do because of where they live and so do Irish people and people from Yorkshire, so how can my mum and others be so disapproving of the Cockney accent?

Ann-Marie Twomey

2. Rewrite the second paragraph in two ways:
   - in the past tense
   - in the third person.

a. It was different when I was with my mum, though.

b. It's different when she's with her mum, though.

25

Standard English

Investigating non-standard forms of English

1. Read these poems which show different types of dialect, slang and colloquial English.

Scotland
from *The Twa Corbies*

Ye'll sit upon his white hause-bane
And I'll pike out his bonny blue een;
And with one lock of his golden hair
We'll theek our nest when it grows bare.

Anon.

```
corbie – crow, raven
een – eyes
hause-bane – collar bone
theek – line
```

England
from *Growing up*

Don't ever mess with Billy
He's a vicious sort of bloke
He'll give you a clout
For saying nowt
And thump you for a joke.

Gareth Owen

England
Excuses

I've writ on the wrong page, Miss,
My pencil went all blunt.
My book was upside-down, Miss.
My book was back to front.

My margin's gone all crooked, Miss.
I've smudged mine with my scarf.
I've rubbed a hole in the paper, Miss.
My ruler's broke in half.

My work's blew out of the window, Miss,
My work's fell in the bin.
The leg's dropped off my chair, Miss,
The ceiling's coming in.

I ate a poison apple, Miss.
I've held a poison pen!
I think I'm being *kidnapped*, Miss!
So… can we start again?

Allan Ahlberg

26

Guyana

from *I like to stay up*

then is when
I does wish
I didn't listen
to no stupid jumbie story

then is when
I does wish
I did read me book instead

Grace Nichols

jumbie – ghost

2. Discuss these poems.
   - In your group, find examples of dialect, slang and colloquial English and turn them into formal standard English
   - Some words have been spelt in such a way that you know they should be said with a special accent. Find some examples.
   - Find some examples of grammar that are not standard English.

3. What would all these extracts lose by being written in standard English? Write your ideas.

The poems have their own 'character' the way they are. It would be boring if all poems were written in the same way.

Verbs

Revising tenses

1. Read this horoscope from a local newspaper.

   Aries *21 March – 20 April*
   You will have sudden good fortune next week – a large sum of money will come your way! Beware of spending it too quickly – you will be wise to save every penny! You will see many friends who will want to help you spend your money – but you will do the sensible thing and look after it carefully. After all, you never know what will be just around the corner!

2. Find out your star sign.
   - Write your own horoscope for next week.
   - It should all be in the future tense.

3. Now write a short recount of last weekend.
   - Include all the important details.
   - It should all be in the past tense.

   Last weekend I went somewhere really interesting. It was …

Verbs

Investigating verb forms

1. Change each verb in these sentences to the form shown in the brackets. Other words will have to be changed around as well.

> **interrogative:** Have you eaten your dinner?
> **imperative:** Eat your dinner, please!
> **active:** I ate my dinner.

The blossom was falling from the tree. (interrogative)

The leaves were being swept up. (imperative)

The leaves were blown by the wind. (active)

The rain began to fall. (interrogative)

Is your umbrella up? (imperative)

The weather forecast was read by John Kettley. (active)

The floods were the worst this century. (interrogative)

Should car drivers go slower in the bad weather? (imperative)

The elderly man was rescued by the local policewoman. (active)

He rewarded her with a piece of his home-made cake (interrogative)

2. Now write three sentences of your own in each of the three forms.

3. Share your sentences with the rest of your group.
   - Are all the verb forms correct?
   - Choose the most interesting sentences to present to the rest of the class.

Verbs

Sorting first, second and third-person verbs

1. The first, second and third-person verbs in this text are all mixed up!
   - Read the text carefully.
   - Notice how the tenses are confused, too!

Ben walk slowly to school. He were worried about the spelling test later that day.

"You am not going to have any problems," said his mother. She say the same thing every week!

"What do she know?" thought Ben to himself, "they am always really hard spellings on a Friday!"

"Hey! Ben!" called Ben's friend Sundip. "How is you?"

"How does you think I are, stupid? It's Friday – spelling test day – don't you remember?"

"Of course I remembers!" cried Sundip. "I have a great idea!"

"What is you thinking of this time?" sighed Ben.

"It are easy! Just learn the spellings every week before the test!"

"Why didn't I think of that?" groaned Ben.

2. Rewrite the text so that it makes sense.
   - Correct all the first, second and third-person verbs.
   - Make sure the tenses are consistent!

3. Now write the next part of the story. Pay close attention to the verbs!

Grammar strategies

Editing and proofreading

1. Here is the first draft of a piece of writing about the invention of the ball-point pen.
   - It is full of interesting information and there are no spelling mistakes.
   - However, there are many grammatical problems that make it difficult to read and understand!

The ball-point pen was invented by Laszlo Biro. Laszlo Biro was born in Hungary. He was the editor of a magazine. He went to a printing works. He got his idea for his new kind of pen. The printers used a kind of quick-drying ink. He thought he could use it in pens. Up until then they used liquid ink from a bottle. It smudged easily. He worked on the design of a new kind of pen. He worked on it for five years. It used a rotating steel ball-point. It had a thin tube to hold the ink.

Laszlo Biro left Europe at the beginning of the Second World War and he went to America and that is where he set up a company to make his ball-point pens and that is where he met an Englishman and he was called Henry Martin and he realised that the new pen would be very useful in the war because it could be used in planes by navigators at high altitudes and ordinary pens did not work very well then and you didn't have to keep filling them up with more ink from a bottle all the time up there.
And we still call ball-point pens biros today because of the man who invented them called Laszlo Biro but he never made much money out of his invention.

2. What grammatical problems can you find in this piece of writing? Think about:
   - words and phrases that could be left out
   - the use of pronouns (is it always clear what noun they refer to?)
   - where sentences are too long or too short.

3. What advice would you give the person who wrote this text?
   Write some short notes explaining the problems and how to avoid them.

4. Rewrite the piece, correcting all the errors you find and making it clear to read.

Grammar strategies

Writing for a younger audience

1. Read the beginning of this fairy tale called *The Golden Goose.*

There was a man who had three sons. The first was called Dummling – which is much the same as Dunderhead, for all thought he was more than half a fool – and he was at all times mocked and ill-treated by the whole household.

It happened that the eldest son took it into his head one day to go into the wood to cut fuel; and his mother gave him a nice pasty and a bottle of wine to take with him, that he might refresh himself at his work. As he went into the wood, a little old man bade him good day and said: "Give me a little piece of meat from your plate, and a little wine out of your bottle, for I am very hungry and thirsty."

But this clever young man said: "Give you my meat and wine? No, I thank you, I should not then have enough left for myself" and away he went. He soon began to cut down a tree; but he had not worked long before he missed his stroke and cut himself, and was forced to go home to have the wound dressed. Now it was the little old man that sent him this mischief.

2. What do you notice about the way this story is written?
   Does anything seem unusual or old-fashioned? Make some notes about:
   - the length of the sentences, and the use of punctuation
   - the choice of words.

3. Imagine that you have the job of rewriting this fairy tale for a book for young children who are still learning to read.
   - What would you need to change?
   - How could you make it simpler and easier to read?

4. Draft a new version of the beginning of *The Golden Goose*.

5. Share and compare your versions.
   - Have you changed the same things?
   - How have you changed them?

Grammar strategies

Writing for an older audience

1. This is the beginning of a story.
   - It is written for very young children who are just beginning to read.
   - To make it easy to read, it is written in very short sentences using only simple, common words.

Polly in the Park

Polly has a dog called Scott.
One day Polly put on Scott's lead.
She took him for a walk.

They went to the park.
They walked past the pond.
They walked past the swings.

Scott saw a squirrel.
He pulled and pulled on his lead.
He pulled very hard.

Polly could not hold on to the lead.
She let go.
Scott ran after the squirrel.

The squirrel ran up a tree.
Scott could see the squirrel.
He barked and barked.

2. Rewrite the story for older children.
   - Use a wider choice of words and longer, more complicated sentences.
   - Add more detail but do not change the plot.

3. Share and compare your versions.

Direct and reported speech

Investigating speech

1. Supergran has amazing powers. One day, she is out rowing in the park with her grandson Willard and a friend when Willard spots someone falling in the water.

2. Tell the story of Supergran's rescue of the girl in words only.
   - What will you need to describe?
   - Will you use direct or reported speech or a mixture of both?

Spoken and written language

Examining differences in language forms

1. Read the following story about a basket-weaver.

Truth is Always Best

A poor basket-weaver was chopping willow branches by the river, when his axe fell into the water. He sat on the bank and cried, and the sound of his tears brought the king of the gods down to help. He dived into the river, and brought back an axe with a golden head. "Is this yours?" he asked.

"No," said the basket-weaver.

The king of the gods threw it back, dived in a second time and brought up an axe with a silver head. "Is this yours?" he asked.

"No," said the basket-weaver.

The king of the gods dived a third time, and brought up an axe with a rusty iron head. "That's mine! Thank you very much!" cried the basket-weaver joyfully.

He ran home excitedly, and told all his neighbours what had happened. Another basket-weaver, a sly, greedy man, rubbed his chin and thought, "There's a fortune to be made from this."

He took an old, rusty axe, went to the river and threw it in. Then he sat on the bank and howled till the king of the gods flew down to help. The king of the gods dived into the river, and brought up an axe with a golden head. At once, the basket-weaver began jumping up and down and shouting, "That's the one! That's the one!"

"It jolly well isn't," said the king of the gods, and tipped the man into the river and gave him a good soaking as a reward for his cheek.

Aesop

2. Capital letters are used in the title and to begin the author's name. Give one other reason why capital letters are used in this story.

3. "That's mine! Thank you very much!"
   Why are exclamation marks used here?

4. Punctuate these words:

   its not fair said the greedy basket-weaver

   How does the punctuation help you understand the meaning?

5. Discuss the differences between spoken and written language.
   - How are the differences shown in this story?
   - Give some examples.

6. Continue the story. Describe what happens when the greedy basket-weaver gets back to his village.
   - Try doing this using role-play in your group.
   - Then produce a short written version of the end of the story.

> Punctuation is used to guide the reader, e.g. exclamation marks to show surprise.

37

Sentence structure

Improving sentences

1. Read these notes that give you some information about three famous British sports stars.

Sharron Davies (swimming)
born in 1962
first swam for England when 10 years old
won silver medal in 1980 Olympic games
became the TV Gladiator, Amazon

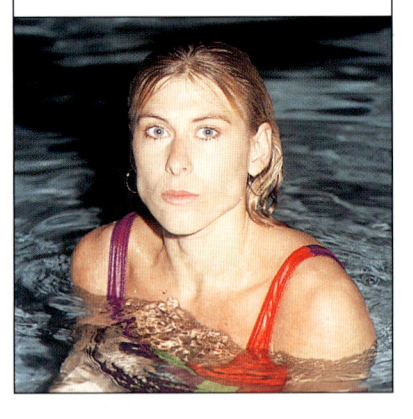

Sally Gunnell (athletics)
born in 1966
started as long jumper
changed to 400m hurdles
won gold medal in 1992 Olympic Games

Chris Boardman (cycling)
born in 1968
rode a revolutionary new bicycle
won gold medal in 1992 Olympics

2. Short notes like this can be helpful, but they can be confusing!
   - Discuss how they could be confusing.
   - How could they be improved?

Such short notes are not always clear, e.g. "changed to 400m hurdles". More detailed sentences could be helpful.

3. Use the notes to write about each of the sports people.
   - First, write two or three sentences that include all the information.
   - Then include as much of the information as you can in just one sentence.

4. Look back at your sentences.
   Can you find other, better ways of giving the information?

38

Sentence structure

Constructing sentences in different ways

1. Read this extract from Ian Serraillier's novel *The Silver Sword*.

   Joseph chose an empty truck and ran alongside at the same speed as the train. Darkness swallowed him. Jan did not see him jump.

   One by one the heavy, dismal, sodden trucks clanked by. Last of all, the small red light, so dim that it hardly showed. Then the shrill note of a whistle, as the train gathered speed beyond the bend.

   It was raining heavily now.
   Jan was soaked to the skin. He hurried away through the dark streets.

   He had tucked the grey cat inside his jacket. It was almost as wet as he was and hardly warm at all. Under his arm he hugged the wooden box. And he thought of the silver sword inside.

2. What do you notice about the way the author organises his ideas in sentences?
   - Find examples of short, simple sentences.
   - Now find examples of longer and more detailed sentences.

3. Now try writing a different version of these events.
   - Keep the information the same.
   - Change the style by structuring the sentences differently.

4. Read through your new version. Does it work as well?

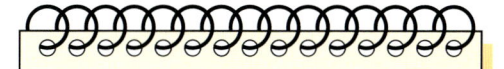

- Short sentences move the action on.
- Longer sentences add detail.

Sentence structure

Adding clauses to sentences

There are problems with the computer in this classroom. Sometimes it deletes the first clause in every sentence written!

1. How do you think these sentences might begin? Complete them by writing the first clause.

_____ because I was late for school.
_____ unless you find your hat.
_____ until he is ten years old.
_____ although it was raining hard.
_____ when I went shopping on Saturday.

2. Sometimes the computer deletes the beginning and the end of each sentence! Complete these sentences by adding clauses.

_____ that I got for Christmas _____
_____ which was on top of the cupboard in my bedroom _____
_____ who dropped his dinner on the floor _____
_____ who is 75 years old _____
_____ which he had been working on for days _____

3. Read through all your sentences to make sure that they make sense and that the clauses fit together.

4. Share and compare your work with the rest of your group.

40

Sentence structure

Using connectives

1. Imagine that a class has been holding a debate about how humans treat animals. Here are some of the things that were said.

> More and more people are refusing to eat meat. This is because...
>
> Most of you seem to be against fox hunting. However,...
>
> There are better ways of controlling the number of foxes. For example,...
>
> Many farmers spray their crops with chemicals to kill insects. As a result...
>
> Some people think it is acceptable to keep endangered animals in zoos. In particular,...

2. What do you think the children went on to say?
   Complete the sentences that have been started above.

3. Write some more pairs of sentences about animal issues.
   Use these connecting words and phrases to begin the second sentence.

For example	Instead	As a result	Also
However	Similarly	Therefore	For this reason

41

Prepositions

Identifying and using prepositions

1. This text tries to persuade people not to go to the circus.

RSPCA campaigns: Don't go to the circus

The RSPCA believes animal circuses are cruel and unnecessary. Although the acts underneath the big top may look glamorous and exciting – behind the spangles and the sparkle is a very different story.

Tamed by fear
Anyone who has seen a circus animal like a lion or tiger respond to the trainer's commands to perform unnatural acts by slinking across the ring with its belly close to the ground, ears flattened and sometimes snarling loudly has seen an animal likely to have been trained by fear.

Trainers often use sticks and sometimes sharp tools like the elephant hook or a walking stick with a nail in the end as a training aid.

On the road
Circus animals are often locked up for long periods of time while they are waiting to travel. They may be kept in the beast wagon from the end of the last evening's performance through the night and through the following day while the equipment is being packed up. The circus then moves on. This could involve a total confinement of over 36 hours. The available space is often less than 2.5 square metres per lion, tiger or leopard.

Please don't go to circuses using animals. Encourage your family and friends to stay away, too!

2. Discuss this text with your group.
   - What are the main arguments put forward by the RSPCA?
   - Do you agree? Why?

3. Answer these questions about prepositions in the text.
   - Is there a preposition in the title? If so, what is it?
   - Find two prepositions in the first paragraph. Write them with the words that go with them.
   - How many different prepositions can you find in the section *Tamed by fear?* Write them in alphabetical order.

4. Read this sentence from the section *On the road.*
   They may be kept in the beast wagon ... while the equipment is being packed up.
   - Is *up* used here as an adverb or as a preposition?
   - Explain your answer.

5. Write two sentences.
   - In the first, use *before* as an adverb.
   - In the second, use *before* as a preposition.

Punctuation revision

Adding punctuation marks

1. Read this text carefully.
   - Some of the punctuation is missing.
   - Some punctuation has been put in the wrong place!

Down: down: down. Would the fall never come to an end!
   "I wonder how many miles I've fallen by this time." she said aloud. "I must be getting somewhere near the centre of the Earth. Let me see: that would be four thousand miles down, I think

   For you see Alice had learnt several things of this sort in her lessons in the schoolroom and thought this was not a very good opportunity for showing off her knowledge. as there was no one to listen to her! still it was good practice to say it over "Yes? that's about the right distance - but then I wonder what latitude or longitude I've got to," Alice had no idea what latitude was or longitude either, but thought they were nice grand words to say,

   Lewis Carroll
   Alice's Adventures in Wonderland

2. Rewrite the text.
   - Correct all the incorrect punctuation.
   - Insert punctuation marks where they are missing.

3. Share your writing with the rest of your group.
   - Is your punctuation the same?
   - What are the differences?

Sometimes there is more than one correct way of punctuating a sentence! Sometimes punctuation is completely wrong!

44

Dialogue

Organising layout of dialogue

1. Read this text about a man talking to a tree. Unfortunately, the dialogue has not been set out in the best or most readable way.

A man went in search of his luck. A tree said to him, "Why are you walking so quickly and staring towards the hills?" The man looked round and saw the tree. "Are you talking to me?" he said. "Yes, I'm talking to you" replied the tree. "Well, I'm looking for my luck. You see I have very bad luck and I want it to change". The tree replied, "Why don't you try the Wise One who lives over the mountain and far away?" "That's a good idea," said the man. "And when you've found him and asked him about your luck," said the tree, "could you ask him why my branches look so ragged and sad and face down to the Earth instead of up to the sky? And why my leaves are brown and shrivelled?" "I can do that for you," said the man. "Goodbye!" The man walked off with a spring in his step. "Good luck!" called the tree.

2. Write out the text again so that the dialogue is easier to read.

Think about:
- Organising the text carefully.
- Starting each new line of dialogue on a new line.

Dialogue

Punctuating dialogue

1. Add punctuation to these sentences, including speech marks.

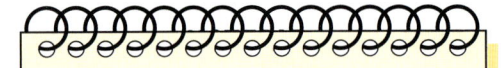

"I've lost it," said Jo.
Jo said, "I've lost it."

Help me I'm slipping said Jim.

The girl said I know I can improve my time in the 100 metres.

I've fallen down the drain the boy shouted loudly.

Leave me alone she cried.

Fish and chips please Darren said.

Look out! The desk's falling the teacher said.

He sobbed I know it's here somewhere.

The weather presenter said There will be showers today.

The leader said Come along tonight.

The assistant said Don't forget your shopping.

2. Now write three dialogue sentences of your own.
   - Punctuate them correctly.
   - Check your work with someone else in your group.

46

Authors

Examining a text from the writer's experience

1. This extract from *The Children of Green Knowe* describes the house as Toseland first sees it.

The entrance hall was a strange place. As they stepped in, a similar door opened at the far end of the house and another man and boy entered there. Then Toseland saw that it was only themselves in a big mirror. The walls round him were partly rough stone and partly plaster, but hung all over with mirrors and pictures and china. There were three big old mirrors all reflecting each other, so that at first Toseland was puzzled to find what was real, and which door one could go through straight, the way one wanted to, not sideways somewhere else. He almost wondered which was really himself.

There were vases everywhere filled with queer flowers – branches of dry winter twigs out of which little tassels and rosettes of flower petals were bursting, some yellow, some white, some purple. They had an exciting smell, almost like something to eat, and they looked as if they had been produced by magic, as if someone had said "Abracadabra! Let these sticks burst into flower." "What if my great-grandmother is a witch!" he thought. Above the vases, wherever there was a beam or an odd corner or a door-post out of which they could, as it were, grow, there were children carved in dark oak, leaning out over the flowers. Most of them had wings, one had a real bird's nest on its head, and all of them had such round polished cheeks they seemed to be laughing and welcoming him.

While he was looking round him, Boggis had taken his coat and cap from him and hung them up. "Your great-grandmother will be in here," he said, and led him to a little old stone doorway such as you might find in a belfry. He knocked on the door. "Come in," said a clear voice. Boggis gave Toseland a shove, and he found himself inside.

Lucy Boston
The Children of Green Knowe

2. Talk about the extract and note your ideas about it.
   - Why do you think the author describes the house in such detail?
   - Which lines suggest the author is describing an actual house?

3. Answer these questions about the text.
   - Which words and sentences make the house sound welcoming and friendly?
   - List the words and sentences that make the house sound strange.
   - What clues are we given about how Toseland feels about coming to the house? What words tell you?
   - Write what you are told about Boggis, and then decide who he might be.

Authors

Investigating the appeal of established authors

1. This is what one 10-year-old boy wrote about an established author.

   I really like reading books by Lewis Carroll. My absolute favourite is *Alice's Adventures in Wonderland*. I like it so much because the characters are so strong and unusual, and so funny! Lewis Carroll creates many different settings in the story – they are so realistic I can just imagine being there. The story is exciting and takes lots of different twists and turns, so you never quite know what is going to happen next. My Dad says he read Lewis Carroll's stories when he was my age!

2. Give three reasons why this boy likes reading Lewis Carroll's stories.

3. Lewis Carroll has appealed to many generations of readers. What clue about this is given in the boy's writing?

4. Discuss the favourite authors of the people in your group.

5. Write a list of the authors, and the main reasons why they are popular.

Think about how the author deals with:
- settings
- characters
- plots

Author	Books written	Why they are popular

Playscripts

Planning a playscript

1. With members of your group, hold a scriptwriters' meeting, following the agenda below.
    - Your aim is to come up with ideas for a new playscript.
    - Your play is to be based on a story or novel you know and like.
    - Choose one person to 'chair' the meeting, and take notes of any decisions taken.

The Agenda

1. What story should we use?

2. Who are the main characters?

3. Which members of the group will write what?

4. Who will be the audience (another class, group, parents)?

5. Where will the story start and end?

6. Any other business?

Note: the meeting must not last more than ten minutes!

2. Write the results of your scriptwriters' meeting.

3. Use your notes to help plan your playscript.
    - Add ideas from other playscripts you have read.
    - Make your notes as detailed as possible.

Playscripts

Evaluating a playscript

1. The Greentown Youth Club have been to see a performance of *Oliver!*
   - Read their opinions carefully.
   - If you have seen *Oliver!*, think about your opinions too!

> Oliver! is about a poor young orphan in Victorian London. It's really sad.

> I thought it was terrible. The acting was bad and the singing was even worse!

> Rubbish!

> The best part was when Oliver asked for more food and the man shouted at him really loudly. I was scared!

> I was really bored. I hate plays and this one must be the worst in the world!

> Brilliant!

2. Talk about all the different opinions here.
   - Two opinions are just one word. Do you think this is a useful way of evaluating the play? Why?
   - Some opinions give evidence from the play. How can this be useful?

3. Now write your own short evaluation of a play you have seen recently or performed in the classroom. Think about:
   - how clearly the words were spoken
   - how smoothly the performance ran
   - how believable the characters were
   - the setting and stage directions.

Remember to use evidence from the performance to back up your opinions!

Characters

Exploring how characters are presented

1. Read what happens next in the story about Buddy and his father at the parents' evening.

"Next please," Mr Normington called.

Buddy took a deep breath and led the way in.

Mr Normington was standing behind his desk. Buddy saw the eyebrows flicker and the smile freeze as he caught sight of his Dad's clothes. There was a brief silence, then Mr Normington pulled himself together.

"Ah, Mr Clark. How do you do?" He held his hand out and Buddy's dad went to shake it with the hand holding the plastic bag. He laughed nervously, put the bag down on Mr Normington's desk, then shook hands.

"Pleased to meet you."

"Yes, well... Do sit down, Mr Clark, and you Buddy. Right, where shall we begin? The reports first, perhaps. Oh." Mr Normington found that all his papers were under the plastic bag. Buddy leaped up and pulled the bag away and Mr Normington began reading the comments that each of the teachers had made. Buddy was so tense that he barely listened, though he was dimly aware that they all sounded quite good. After every subject report, Mr Normington stopped and looked at Buddy's dad who kept saying, "Oh, nice."

Nigel Hinton
Buddy

2. What do you learn from this extract about the three characters?

3. Write some statements about how each of them feels about this situation and about the other people.

Buddy feels ...
His father feels ...
Mr Normington feels ...

4. Now think about how the author has given you this information.
   - Think about what the characters do and say.
   - Provide evidence from the text for each of your statements.

what I think	evidence from text

5. Work with two partners to plan and present a role-play performance of this scene.
   - Make the characters' words and actions show how they feel.
   - Continue the scene.

Characters

Writing new characters

1. Imagine that when Buddy leaves Mr Normington's classroom with his father he meets his new friend Owen Bennett in the corridor.
   Read the Fact File on Owen.

FACT FILE

Name	Owen Dominic Bennett
Age	11
Members of family	lives with his mother; only child
Appearance	tall for his age; strong and fit; fashionable hair cut
Important events	captain of school football team; winner of North of England Under-11s Chess Championships
Relationships	likes to be with people who he feels are his equal; tends to ignore other peoples' feelings; no long-lasting friendships; currently friends with Buddy Clark
Personality	very sure of himself; can be conceited and selfish

2. What do you think will happen when Owen meets Buddy and his father? What do you think they will say to each other?

3. Plan and write the scene.
   - Use the information in the Fact File on Owen and what you know about Buddy and his father from the earlier scenes.
   - Think about how to use action and dialogue to convey the characters' feelings.

Structure

Examining story openings

1. Read this opening paragraph from *Bella's Den*.

We always came down to the lane on our horses. We galloped faster and faster, mud flying round us and Polly leaping behind. We had to rein the horses in really hard when we got to the farm gate in case they tried to leap over and send us flying. Then we tethered them to the fence. Bella's was called Cowboy and mine was called Jet. We had to leave them at the fence because they'd never make it through the next bit. They weren't really horses, you see. They were bikes.

Berlie Doherty
Bella's Den

2. Discuss this paragraph with the rest of your group.
   - What kind of impression do you think the author is trying to give in this paragraph?
   - What makes this an unusual introduction to a story?
   - What kind of characters do you think are being introduced here?

3. The opening of this story is written as a piece of action.
   - Rewrite it as dialogue between the two characters.
   - Think carefully about what they will say, and how they will say it.
   - Try to give the same impressions as the original paragraph.

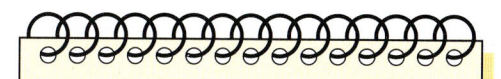

"Let's go down the lane on our horses, like we always do!" cried Bella.

Structure

Examining story structures

1. This list of events from *Bella's Den* in the Anthology is all mixed up. Look at the list carefully.

Examining the den.	Finding Bella's path to the den.
Riding down the lane quickly on their bikes.	Scrambling and rolling down the path.

   - Rewrite these points in the correct order.
   - Add any other details you think are important.

2. Which do you think is the most important point from this list? Why?

3. Talk about what you think might happen in the rest of the story.
   - Think carefully about how the events will be linked together.
   - Which will be the most important event?
   - What other events will happen to the two girls to make the story interesting?
   - How will it all end?

4. Together, write a list of points or draw a diagram to show the main events and the ending.
   Show clearly how all the events link together!

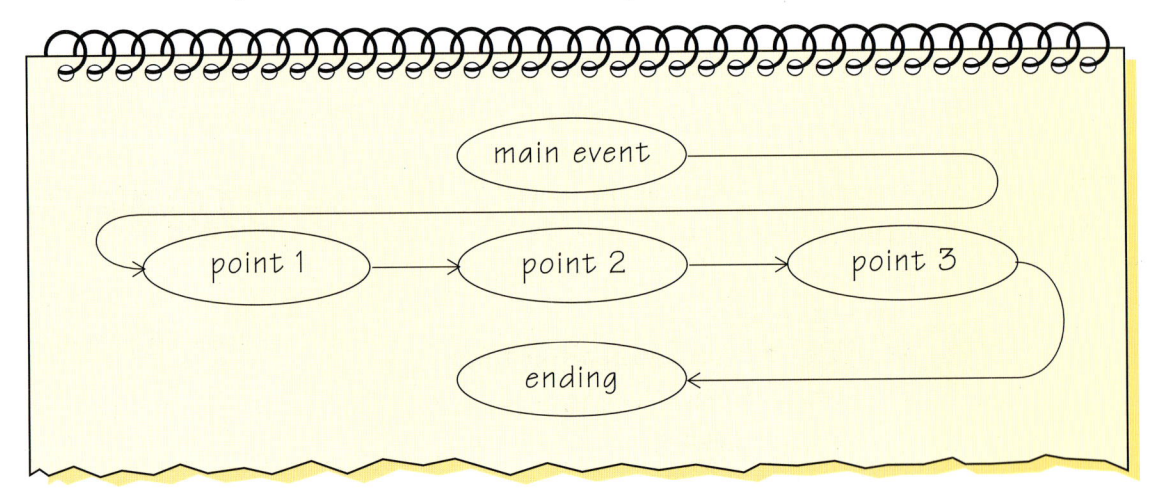

   main event

   point 1 → point 2 → point 3

   ending

56

Structure

Comparing important episodes

1. These are extracts from important moments in two stories: *Bella's Den* and *The True Story of the Three Little Pigs*.

A It was a fox. He seemed to grow out of the darkness of the hole, and then took shape as the moon lit him. He stood as if he had been turned to stone, and he was staring right at our den, right through the leaf strands, right at me. He was locked right into me, reading the thoughts in my mind, and I daren't move or breathe, I daren't do anything but stare back at him, till my eyes were blurring. I thought I would pass out with holding myself so still, and my skin was ice-cold, frozen cold with fear.

Berlie Doherty
Bella's Den

B I knocked on the brick house. No answer.
   I called "Mr Pig, Mr Pig, are you in?"
   And do you know what that rude little porker answered?
   "Get out of here, Wolf. Don't bother me again."
   Talk about impolite!
   He probably had a whole sackful of sugar.
   And he wouldn't give me even one little cup for my dear sweet old granny's birthday cake.
   What a pig!

I was just about to go home and make a nice birthday card instead of a cake, when I felt a cold coming on.

    I huffed.

    And I snuffed.

    And I sneezed once again.

    Then the Third Little Pig yelled, "And your old granny can sit on a pin!"

Jon Scieszka
The True Story of the Three Little Pigs

2. Do you think the narrators are trying to influence you or change your opinion?
   - Why are they telling you about each incident?
   - Which extract includes the most detail or description?
   - Which extract includes the most events?
   - Which story is told the quickest?
   - Why is this?

3. The two stories are trying to have very different effects on the reader.
   - How do the writers of *Bella's Den* and *The True Story of the Three Little Pigs* want you to react to their texts?
   - Why do you think this? Discuss with the rest of your group.

Reading strategies

Examining details in a text

1. Read this text from *The Runaway Summer* by Nina Bawden.

Mary said, "Grampy, when am I going home?"

Her grandfather said, "Don't you like it here?"

Mary wriggled her shoulders and sucked at a strand of hair as if she found this a difficult question to answer, though in fact it shouldn't have been, and not only because it was pleasant to live near the sea instead of in London. Mary was fond of her grandfather – as fond as she was of anyone, that is – and he and Aunt Alice were always at home and never left her by herself in the evenings as her father and mother sometimes did. She had found it was comforting to hear voices downstairs when you were lying awake in bed. Particularly when you knew that these voices would never get loud and shout at each other.

In fact, Mary could have said, "Yes, I do like being here." But she always found it hard to say she liked anything, just as she found it almost impossible to say "Thank you," or "I'm sorry". Sometimes she wanted to, but the words stuck in her throat, like pills. So all she said was, "Oh, it's all right, I suppose. I don't even want to go home, really. It's just that I want to know when I *am* going."

Her grandfather poked in the rose bed with this stick and found another weed. "I don't know." He looked at her sadly. "I'm sorry, Mary."

She stared at the rose bushes. "You mean they're not coming back for me?"

Nina Bawden
The Runaway Summer

2. What evidence is there that Mary's parents quarrelled a lot?

3. Why does Mary like living at her grandfather's? Give all the reasons you can find.

4. What additional information do you learn about Mary in this extract?

5. *Sometimes ... the words stuck in her throat, like pills.*
    - Do you think this is a good description?
    - Give your reasons.

6. How do you think Mary feels at the end of the extract?

7. What evidence is there in the text that Mary keeps her feelings to herself?

8. Why do you think Mary asks her grandfather when she is going home?

9. Why do you think that Mary's grandfather looks at her sadly at the end of the extract?

Traditional stories

Exploring text features

1. This is how six well-known stories begin. Two are myths, two are fables, and two are legends.

A

A tortoise and a hare got into an argument about which of them could run the faster.

B

In the Dreamtime, when the world was still in the making, the Ancient Sleepers rose from their beds and walked across sea and land, shaping the rocks, the plants, the creatures, arranging the stars to please the eye.

C

Thousands of years ago, on the island of Crete, there lived a terrible monster called the Minotaur. It was half man and half bull, and it lived at the centre of the Labyrinth – a vast underground maze. One day, a young Greek prince called Theseus heard about this terrible beast.

61

D

Long ago, before humans first walked on the earth, the Sun and Moon lived together in Africa as man and wife.

E

A dog was lying asleep in a farmyard when he was suddenly attacked by a wolf.

F

There was once a boy – the son of the Red King – who had the ambition to live forever and never grow old. So he said to his father, "Give me a horse and my inheritance, and I shall travel the world till I find what I am seeking."

2. Talk about each extract with your group.
   - Decide which are myths, which are legends and which are fables.
   - Make brief notes about your ideas.

3. Write a note about each of these stories, explaining why you think it is a myth, fable or legend.

4. Choose two of the stories and think about what might happen next.
   - What do you think the story is going to be about?
   - What do you think might happen? Why?

Story:
What it is about:
What might happen next:

Traditional stories

Comparing different versions of a story

1. This is the beginning of a Scottish version of *Cinderella* called *Rushen Coatie*.

   There was once a king and a queen, as many a one has been; few have we seen, and as few may we see. But the queen died, leaving only one bonny girl, and she told her on her deathbed: "My dear, after I am gone, there will come to you a little red calf, and whenever you want anything, speak to it, and it will give it to you."

   Now, after a while, the king married again an ill-natured wife with three ugly daughters of her own. And they hated the king's daughter because she was so bonny. So they took all her fine clothes away from her, and gave her only a coat made of rushes. So they called her Rushen Coatie, and made her sit in the kitchen nook, amid the ashes. And when dinner-time came, the nasty stepmother sent her out a thimbleful of broth, a grain of barley, a thread of meat, and a crumb of bread.

2. Compare this version of *Cinderella* with the usual version and with *Wishbones*, the version in the Anthology.
   - Think about the setting of the story, the characters and the plot.
   - Use a chart like this to record the differences.

	Rushen Coatie	Cinderella	Wishbones
setting			
characters			
plot			

3. Write a short note giving your ideas on the similarities and differences between each of the stories.

4. How do you think *Rushen Coatie* is going to continue? Write an outline plan to show what you think will happen.

Traditional stories

Examining alternative story-telling

1. This is the beginning of a modern fairy tale called *The Practical Princess* by Jay Williams.

   Princess Bedelia was as lovely as the moon shining upon a lake full of waterlilies. She was as graceful as a cat leaping. And she was also extremely practical.
   When she was born, three fairies had come to her cradle to give her gifts as was usual in that country. The first fairy had given her beauty. The second had given her grace. But the third, who was a wise old creature, had said: "I give her common sense."
   "I don't think much of that gift," said King Ludwig, raising his eyebrows. "What good is common sense to a princess? All she needs is charm."
   Nevertheless, when Bedelia was eighteen years old, something happened which made the king change his mind.
   A dragon moved into the neighbourhood.

2. What other fairy tales does this remind you of? Why?
   Write a list, giving your reasons.

3. What is unusual and surprising about the beginning of *The Practical Princess*?

4. Write a back page advertising blurb for the story.
   Try to get people excited about how different and special it is.

   > The Practical Princess is a strange and fascinating tale …

5. The rest of the story is just as unusual as the beginning.
   - What do you think happens?
   - Write a plan or a short description (synopsis) showing how the story might continue and what might happen at the end.

Traditional stories

Writing a fable

1. These are some morals from Aesop's fables.

   Be happy with what you've got.

   United we stand; divided we fall.

   A wise man learns from his mistakes.

   Selfishness brings its own punishment.

   Don't try to be something you are not.

   Persuasion is often more effective than force.

2. Plan your own fable to illustrate one of these morals. Think about:
   - What ideas and personalities you need for your story.
   - Which animals these ideas and personalities are usually linked to.
   - Decide which animals will be in your fable.

   fox – cunning
   ant – hard-working

3. Draft your fable.
   - What events can you use to illustrate the moral?
   - Keep the action in your fable very simple.

4. Read your draft.
   - Is it short, simple and clear?
   - If you need to, make some improvements.

65

Traditional stories

Writing a legend

1. This is a description of a fantastical beast called a *basilisk*.

The basilisk

The basilisk is hatched by a serpent from a cockerel's egg. It has the scaly body and wings of a dragon with the beak and head of a cockerel. Known sometimes as the King of the Serpents, it wears a crown on its head.

One look from a basilisk's fiery eyes causes death and destruction: human beings and animals fall down dead; grass burns; fruit rots; water becomes poisoned or dries up.

People try to protect themselves from the basilisk by carrying a mirror to turn its deadly gaze back upon itself.

2. Plan and draft a legend featuring this fantastical creature.
   - Where will the story happen?
   - How will the basilisk appear?
   - What damage will it do?
   - Will it be defeated? If so, how?

How will it be defeated?
- By a hero or heroine?
- By a simple, ordinary person?
- By strength or by cunning?

Point of view

Exploring point of view

1. Read this imaginary letter written to the Big Bad Wolf by a solicitor representing Little Red Riding Hood.

> Meeny, Mino, Mo & Co, Solicitors
> Alley O Building, Toe Lane Tel: 12345.
>
> Dear Mr Wolf,
>
> We are writing to you on behalf of our client, Miss Riding-Hood, concerning her grandma. Miss Hood tells us that you are presently occupying her grandma's cottage and wearing her grandma's clothes without this lady's permission.
>
> Please understand that if this harassment does not cease, we will call in the Official Woodcutter, and – if necessary – all the King's horses and all the King's men.
>
> On a separate matter, we must inform you that Messrs Three Little Pigs Ltd, are now firmly resolved to sue for damages. Your offer of shares in a turnip or apple-picking business is declined, and all this huffing and puffing will get you nowhere.
>
> Yours sincerely,
> H Meeny

Janet and Alan Ahlberg
The Jolly Postman

2. Answer these questions.
   - Why is Harold Meeny writing to the Big Bad Wolf?
   - What sort of letter is it?
   - What do you need to know to understand this letter properly?

3. Whose point of view is shown in this letter?

4. How is this different to the way *Little Red Riding Hood* is usually told?

Point of view

Investigating alternative points of view

1. Read this extract from the end of *The True Story of the Three Little Pigs*.

   I huffed.
   And I snuffed.
   And I sneezed once again.
   Then the Third Pig yelled, "And your old granny can sit on a pin!"
   Now I'm usually a pretty calm fellow. But when somebody talks about my granny like that, I go a little crazy.
   When the cops drove up, of course I was trying to break down this Pig's door.
   And the whole time I was huffing and puffing and sneezing and making a real scene.
   The rest, as they say, is history.
   The news reporters found out about the two pigs I had for dinner. They figured a sick guy going to borrow a cup of sugar didn't sound very exciting.
   So they jazzed up the story with all that "Huff and puff and blow your house down".
   And they made me the Big Bad Wolf.
   That's it.
   The real story. I was framed.
   But maybe you could loan me a cup of sugar.

2. What point of view is this part of the story told from?

3. How do you know this? Use evidence from the text.

4. Do you think the wolf is telling the truth? Give reasons for your answer.

5. What point of view is this story usually told from?

6. How does the wolf's version of events make you feel about this story? Why?

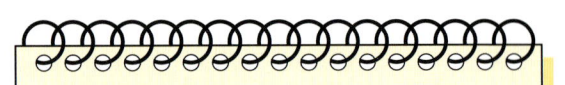

> I still prefer the original version of the story, because it is more exciting!

68

Point of view

Changing point of view

1. Discuss the different versions of *The Three Little Pigs* you have explored in this unit:
   - the traditional version, told from the pigs' point of view
   - the alternative version, told from the wolf's point of view.

2. Make brief notes about what you like or dislike about each version.

3. You are going to plan, draft and write your own version of the story, from a completely different point of view. You could:
   - write a version of the story in the same style, told by a different character, e.g. one of the pigs' neighbours
   - write the story in a different form, e.g. as a letter or an e-mail
   - change the setting of the story completely, as well as the point of view, e.g. set it in outer space.

4. Plan your version of the story in note form.
   - Be clear about the point of view of your story.
   - Include a list of the main events, in order.
   - Add details about the characters and setting.
   - How will your version of the story end?

The Three Pigs in Space
- 3 pigs trapped on an alien planet
- Each trying to build a spaceship to escape
- Story told by an alien
- Big bad wolf has crashed on the planet
- He plans to steal one of the ships when it is finished — but which one?

Genres

Identifying different genres

1. Which of these extracts come from the same book? Match the three pairs.

A

Dozens of killer animals were watching me, plotting something awful against the city boy who slept in the Death Room.

B

Carole was fibbing to Kate. She wasn't having any trouble with this at all on her pony, but she wanted to get Kate involved, even if only on the telephone. Carole knew that there were a lot of ways to get a horse to lengthen his stride, and that Kate would have lots of ideas for her.

C

"You're jolly mean, Ranni," said Jack, but he knew Ranni of old. There was nothing for it but to promise.

"All right – we won't go down the abandoned shafts again," he said, sulkily.

D

I didn't know what it was. But I knew it was coming directly at me!

It was flying straight at my face!

It had long, fierce claws that looked like a dozen daggers. And all the claws were extended, gleaming in the moonlight, trying to rip out my eyes!

E

Carole and Stevie were practically bursting with curiosity by the time they sat down together on the knoll overlooking Samson's paddock. They waited expectantly while Lisa removed the foil top from her yoghurt and opened up her fruit juice.

F

Jack was looking in the big chest they had hauled away from the door. "I'd like to know what makes it so heavy," he said. "We almost couldn't drag it away. Look – rugs – cloth of some kind – and what's this in the bottom drawer of the chest, wrapped up in blue curtains?"

2. Each of these books comes from a particular kind of popular fiction.
   - What do you think each one is? How do you know?
   - What kind of things might happen in the story?
   - Record your ideas in a chart like this.

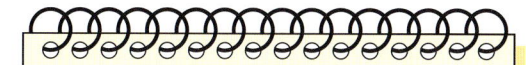

Possible genres could be:
horror   detective
adventure   horse/pony
fantasy   humour

Extracts	Type of fiction, with evidence	Things that might happen

Genres

Investigating ghost stories

1. Read this back-cover blurb for a story in the *Goosebumps* series.

2. What do you think might happen in this story?
   - What characters might be in the story as well as Jerry?
   - Invent an important, exciting, scary episode (you could use the photocopiable planner).

Goosebumps: Ghost Beach

Jerry can't wait to explore the dark, scary old cave he's found down by the beach. Especially when he hears about the ghost. And starts finding the strange little skeletons.

Everyone tells Jerry it could be dangerous to go into the cave. But he can't help wondering. Is there really a ghost in there? Or is it just a stupid story?

Jerry knows there's only one way to find out. And *nobody's* going to stop him exploring that cave. But maybe he's making a really big mistake – because it's *seriously* spooky in there…

ISBN 0-590-13545-7
UK £3.99
SCHOLASTIC

3. Write a draft of this episode. Think about:
   - what's important in this kind of story:
     - the action
     - the atmosphere
   - the way in which stories like this are written:
     - the kind of sentences
     - the kind of descriptions.

4. When you have finished your first draft, read it through carefully. Look for ways of increasing the suspense and making it more scary.

Genres

Writing in a genre

1. This is the back cover of a book in a series called *Scrambled Legs*. The title of this book is *Save D.A.D.*

2. What do you think might happen in this story?
   - Invent an important episode – the most exciting moment or a turning-point.
   - What part will each of the five children have in this episode?
   - Make sure they talk and act 'in character'.
   - What atmosphere do you want to create (e.g. comic, exciting)?

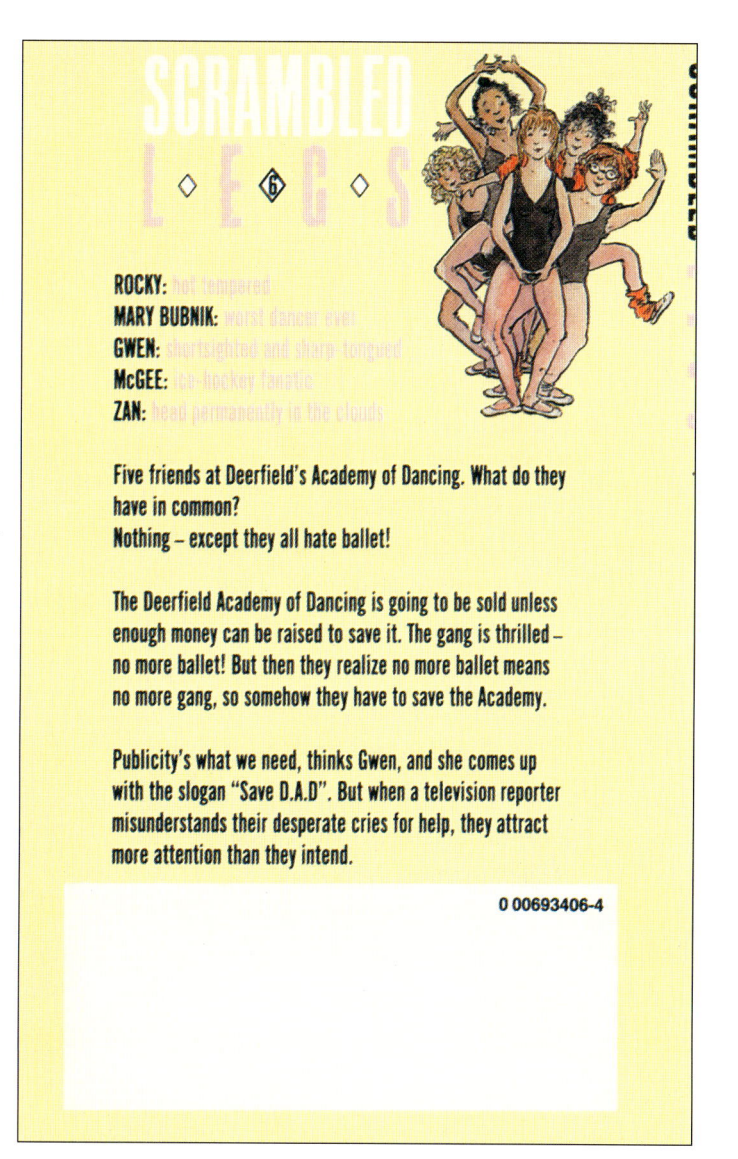

SCRAMBLED LEGS

ROCKY: hot-tempered
MARY BUBNIK: worst dancer ever
GWEN: shortsighted and sharp-tongued
McGEE: ice-hockey fanatic
ZAN: head permanently in the clouds

Five friends at Deerfield's Academy of Dancing. What do they have in common?
Nothing – except they all hate ballet!

The Deerfield Academy of Dancing is going to be sold unless enough money can be raised to save it. The gang is thrilled – no more ballet! But then they realize no more ballet means no more gang, so somehow they have to save the Academy.

Publicity's what we need, thinks Gwen, and she comes up with the slogan "Save D.A.D". But when a television reporter misunderstands their desperate cries for help, they attract more attention than they intend.

0 00693406-4

3. Write a draft of this episode.

4. When you have finished your first draft, read it through carefully. Think about:
   - the action
   - the atmosphere
   - the characters
   - the dialogue.

5. Discuss ways of improving your draft.

73

Cultures and traditions

Exploring different cultures and traditions

1. Read this text about Neetu's and Sanjay's visit to see their grandparents in Calcutta.

"I'll need extra milk today," Grandma Chatterji told the milkman happily. "My daughter and her family are visiting from England. They arrive today!"

The milkman lifted the huge churn of milk from his head and measured out a cataract of white milk into Grandma's pail.

"It's nearly time to go!" announced Uncle Ashok from the veranda. "Where's Grandpa?"

"I don't know," answered Radha, as Sassu oiled her hair till it shone inky black and then deftly divided and plaited it tightly, so that not one strand would stick out.

"I can't see him," shouted Rahul from the roof where he had gone to fly his kite.

"He didn't come this way," muttered Aunty Meena as she crouched over the beautiful welcoming rangoli pattern she was sprinkling outside the front gate.

"I'm going to hail a taxi," said Uncle Ashok, "and if Grandpa doesn't turn up, we'll just have to leave without him."

He stood on the edge of the pavement, just between the paan seller and the pavement barber. Cars and cows and buses and rickshaws all rushed by.

Then suddenly, a voice rang out, "Come on, all of you! Get in. We're going to be late!"

"Grandpa!" everyone shouted.

It was very crowded at the airport and they had to wait a such a long time. As passengers began coming out with all their bags and suitcases, Radha and Rahul looked and looked to see if they could recognise their cousins, as they had only ever seen them in photographs. Then, suddenly, there was a family who looked Indian, but who wore western clothes.

"Didi, Didi, Didi!" cried Aunty Meena, rushing towards her older sister. Then what a lot of hugging and kissing and a fierce pinching of cheeks there was. Neetu and Sanjay's mother and father both bent down respectfully and touched the feet of Grandpa and Grandma Chatterji.

"Welcome to Calcutta!" beamed Grandpa, draping their necks with garlands.

Jamila Gavin
Grandpa's Indian Summer

2. Describe all the ways in which their relations prepare to welcome Neetu and Sanjay and their parents.

3. It is Neetu's and Sanjay's very first visit to India. What unusual sights will they see in the busy street outside their grandfather's house?

4. What will Neetu and Sanjay notice is different about the way milk is delivered in Calcutta?

5. Describe in your own words the excited meeting at the airport.

6. Why did Neetu's and Sanjay's parents touch the feet of Grandpa and Grandma Chatterji?

7. Would you like to read the book from which this extract comes?
    - Discuss this in your group.
    - Give reasons for your answer.

Cultures and traditions

Investigating a well-known story

1. Read this extract from *The Adventures of Tom Sawyer*.

Ben said: "Say, I'm going in a-swimming, I am. Don't you wish you could? But of course you'd rather work, wouldn't you?"

Tom contemplated the boy a bit, and said:

"What do you call work?"

"Why, ain't that work?"

Tom resumed his whitewashing, and answered carelessly:

"Well, maybe it is, and maybe it ain't. All I know is, it suits Tom Sawyer."

"Oh, come now, you don't mean to let on that you like it?"

The brush continued to move.

"Like it? Well, I don't see why I oughtn't to like it. Does a boy get a chance to whitewash a fence every day?"

That put the thing in a new light. Ben stopped nibbling his apple. Tom swept his brush daintily back and forth – stepped back to note the effect – added a touch here and there – criticised the effect again – Ben watching every move, and getting more and more interested, more and more absorbed. Presently he said:

"Say, Tom, let me whitewash a little."

"No, no; I reckon it wouldn't hardly do, Ben. You see Aunt Polly's awful particular about this fence; it's got to be done very careful; I reckon there ain't one boy in a thousand, maybe two thousand, that can do it the way it's got to be done."

"Oh, come now. I'd let you, if you was me, Tom. I'll give you the core of my apple."

"No, Ben; now don't; I'm afeard –"

"I'll give you all of it!"

Tom gave up the brush.

Mark Twain
The Adventures of Tom Sawyer

2. Do you think that Ben is one of Tom's best friends? Explain your answer.

3. How does Tom trick Ben into doing his work for him?

4. What adjectives would you use to describe Tom Sawyer?

5. The story is set in America. How can you guess this from the way the boys talk?

6. Can you guess what will happen as other boys arrive?

7. Mark Twain wrote this book over 120 years ago.
   - Does the extract seem old-fashioned in any way?
   - Do you think boys have changed much since this story was written?

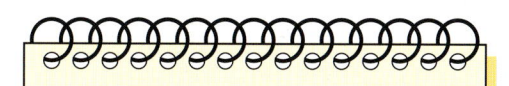

Some of the words they use are old-fashioned.

Forms of poetry

Examining and responding to a poem

1. Read Gareth Owen's poem *Excuses, excuses!*

Excuses, excuses!
Late again Blenkinsopp?
What's the excuse this time?
Not my fault sir.
Whose fault is it then?
Grandma's sir.
Grandma's? What did she do?
She died sir.
Died?
She's seriously dead alright sir.
That makes four grandmothers
    this term Blenkinsopp
And all on P.E. days
I know. It's very upsetting sir.
How many grandmothers have
    you got Blenkinsopp?
Grandmothers sir? None sir.
You said you had four.
All dead sir.
And what about yesterday
    Blenkinsopp?
What about yesterday sir?
You were absent yesterday.
That was the dentist sir.
The dentist died?
No sir, My teeth sir.
You missed the maths test
    Blenkinsopp!
I'd been looking forward to it sir.
Right, line up for P.E.
Can't sir.
No such word as 'can't'
    Blenkinsopp.
No kit sir.
Where is it?
Home sir.
What's it doing at home?

Not ironed sir.
Couldn't you iron it?
Can't sir.
Why not?
Bad hand sir.
Who usually does it?
Grandma sir.
Why couldn't she do it?
Dead sir.

Gareth Owen

2. How many different excuses can you count in the poem?

3. How does Gareth Owen make this poem sound like a conversation?

4. Is this poem meant to be funny or serious? Use evidence from the poem in your answer.

5. Prepare a reading aloud of the poem.
   - Practise it carefully first
   - You could take parts and read it like a conversation.

6. Brainstorm with your group as many good excuses (real or made-up) as you can think of.

7. Choose six of them and write a group poem about excuses.

The dog ate my homework.
Aliens landed in the garden.
Dad's car broke down.

Classic poetry

Writing new verses of a poem

1. Read the first verse of Ogden Nash's poem *The Adventures of Isabel*.

   Isabel met an enormous bear;
   Isabel, Isabel, didn't care.
   The bear was hungry, the bear was ravenous,
   The bear's big mouth was cruel and cavernous.
   The bear said, Isabel, glad to meet you,
   How do, Isabel, now I'll eat you!
   Isabel, Isabel, didn't worry,
   Isabel didn't scream or scurry.
   She washed her hands and she
      straightened her hair up,
   Then Isabel quietly ate the bear up.

   - There are three more verses in the poem.
   - Each tells the story of a similar adventure in which Isabel defeats a character that threatens her: she drinks a witch; she cuts off a giant's head; she cures a troublesome doctor.
   - Each verse has the same pattern. Lines 7 and 8 are repeated in all the verses.

2. Write a new verse for the poem.
   - First, decide what will happen.
   - Who will Isabel meet? What will this character look like? How will it threaten her?
   - What will it say? How will she defeat it?
   - Use the language patterns of the first verse, and repeat lines 7 and 8.

   > She could meet an alien monster, or her worst teacher, or a huge hungry spider!

Classic poetry

Exploring imagery in poems

1. Read these two poems that children have written about animals. They begin by comparing the animal with something else.

The crab

There you lie,
Buried in sand.
An armoured vehicle,
In your desert camouflage.
You move stealthily,
Like a tank,
Sideways.

Gordon Cullingford

The bat

The bat is...
Scrumpled-up brown fabric,
With bin liner wings.
Swooping swiftly, but silently
Through the dark forbidding trees.
The bat is the highwayman of the forest.

Rachel Charlotte Minton

2. List all the things to which the poets compare the crab and the bat.

3. Choose an animal. Write a list of things it is like.
   - Think about how it moves.
   - Describe its appearance.
   - What sounds does it make?

4. Use these ideas to help you write a poem about the animal.

Recounted texts

Sorting different kinds of text

1. Some of these extracts are from chronological recounts. Some are not. Which is which?

A	• Break three eggs into a bowl. • Add some salt and pepper and a tablespoonful of milk. • Beat the eggs with a fork until the yolks and whites are well mixed.	B	When strong winds blow on to a sandy beach, the sand is piled up into dunes. These can be 30 metres high. The wind moves the dunes inland.	C	*Herring Gull* The most common large British gull, found all round the coast. Nests on all kinds of coast, and in winter often comes inland to feed.
D	Suddenly, the noise stopped. I was just about to go, when I saw a door open. A man carrying something heavy stepped out into the street. He was soon followed by another man carrying a bag.	E	When dawn broke, the sailors saw a small island ahead of them. As Columbus prepared to land, a group of people came out of the forest.	F	One day, I arrived on the peak and found a small group of chimps just below me in the upper branches of a thick tree. As I watched, I saw that one of them was holding a piece of meat.

2. Draw up a table like this and sort the extracts into two groups by writing the letters in the correct column.

chronological recounts	other kinds of writing

3. Write a short note about each extract.
    • Explain what kind of writing it is.
    • How can you tell?

Recounted texts

Examining a text closely

1. Read this account of Columbus's landing in the New World.

On 11 October, several land birds were seen flying around the masts of Columbus's ships and a piece of wood carved into a strange shape was fished out of the sea. Columbus was convinced that land was not far away. By dusk nothing had been seen, but Columbus ordered the ships to drop anchor in case they ran aground in the dark.

At ten that night, Columbus saw a light to the south-west. He pointed the light out to crew members Pedro Guttierrez and Rodrigo Sanchez, who both saw it. The Pinta pushed forwards in the direction of the light. At two o'clock in the morning of 12 October, a sailor named Rodrigo de Triana sighted land. When he heard the news, Columbus fell to his knees. He had found land where he had been told there was none.

When dawn broke, the sailors saw a small island ahead of them. As Columbus prepared to land, a group of people came out of the forest. They stood on the beach and stared at the ships. Columbus, the Pinza brothers and a large group of sailors clambered into boats to land and claim the island for Spain. Columbus had dressed in his finest suit. When he saw the people on shore, he buckled on his armour and sword in case there was trouble.

In the early morning light Columbus and his men stepped ashore. Watching the crowd nervously, they unfurled the flag of Spain and Columbus proclaimed himself viceroy of the island.

Columbus then approached the group of people, keeping a grip on his sword in case they were dangerous. In fact they were friendly. They were amazed by the ships and clothes of the Spaniards. When Columbus gave them a few trinkets, they seemed very happy. Then they ran off.

Rupert Matthews
The Voyage of Columbus

2. Write a short note explaining the key idea for each of these five paragraphs.

3. Draw and label a time-line showing these events.

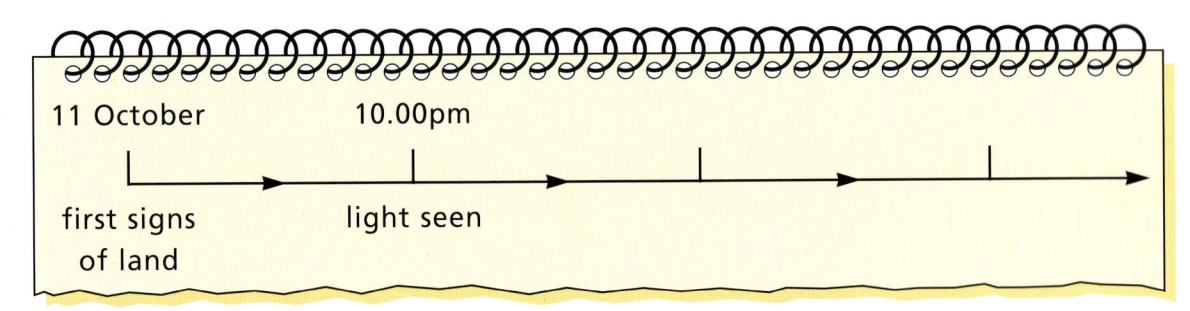

11 October   10.00pm

first signs of land   light seen

Recounted texts

Writing a recount from notes

1. These are the notes that PC Sue Travis scribbled in her pad as she continued to follow the thieves from the Art Gallery.

	SATURDAY 19TH JUNE 1999 DUTY AKM44 5.30 – 6.30
5.37	second man throws bag over wall – clanking noise – tools?
	picks up parcel – walks on – struggling with weight of it
5.40	hear running footsteps
	men hide in doorway – PC SHEIKH comes round corner
	first man jumps out – knocks him over
5.42	radio station for ambulance
	white van K249 MTX stops by doorway
	man jumps out - all three put parcel in back
	van races off high speed
5.45	radio number to station
	go to tend PC SHEIKH

2. Imagine that you are PC Travis.
   - Back at the Police Station, you write your report of what happened that night.
   - Make sure your report is clear and that everything is in the correct order.

3. Share your first draft with the rest of your group.
   - Have you included all the details correctly?
   - How could your report be improved?

Recounted texts

Writing a recount from diary entries

1. Read these notes that an imaginary explorer made in his diary.

Tuesday 7th June
Water supplies very low. Men in poor spirits. Muttering that the voyage is doomed. A bad day.

Wednesday 8th June
Land sighted just before sunset – at last! A small island. Men's spirits lift. Prepare to go ashore tomorrow. Load rowing boat with empty barrels. Must find fresh water. Decide not to tell crew that we are lost.

Thursday 9th June
Row ashore at first light with Percival and Foskett. White sand. Tall coconut trees. F. climbs tree and throws down coconuts. Quench our thirst with the sweet cool coconut milk. Set off towards hills in search of water. Walk till nightfall. Do not find any. Sleep in mouth of cave. Dare not go inside for fear of animals. Worried about men back on ship.

Friday 10th June
Awake before sunrise. Climb to top of large rock. See sparkling in distance. A stream! Wake P and F and run to the stream. Jump into the pure, cold water and drink our fill. What joy! Light fire to signal success to ship. Fetch barrels from beach and fill and load into rowing boat. Back to ship before sunset. Great cheers from the men.

Later, when he got safely home, the explorer used these notes to help him write an account of his journeys and adventures.

2. Write an account for 7th to 10th June.
   - Use your imagination to fill in more detail!
   - Make sure the events are recounted in the order in which they happened and are clearly linked together.

Instructions

Following and evaluating instructions

1. Look at these instructions for making a Bee Hide in your garden.

   YOU WILL NEED
   - A medium-sized plant pot (about 15cm across)
   - Pet mouse bedding material (from pet shops)
   - A small piece of hosepipe, or large stones/piece of slate

   a. Make sure the hole in the bottom of the pot is at least 20mm across.

   b. If you have a piece of hosepipe, push this in the hole of the plant pot.

   c. Loosely fill the pot with the mouse bedding.

   d. Dig a hole deep enough to take the pot in a sunny bank or a sunny area of rough grass (not the lawn unless you have permission!)

   e. Bury the pot, upside down in the hole. Either cut off the pipe so it is level with the ground, or arrange the stones and/or slate as shown in the drawing, so that they protect the entrance from rain and allow bees to get in and out.

   f. Watch from a distance (bees sting!) to see the bees arrive and nest in your bee hide.

2. Do you think this is a good text for explaining how to do something?
   - What makes it good or not?
   - Write four features that make it easy or difficult to read or understand.

3. Discuss your ideas with the rest of your group.
   - Do you all agree?
   - Use your ideas to write a list of questions to use when reading other instructional texts.

87

Instructions

Writing instructions

1. Mrs McNulty's new class have been asked to write some instructions.
   - They need to help younger children with some tasks.
   - Look carefully at the range of instructions needed.
   - These are harder to explain than you might think!

Tying shoelaces

Swimming breaststroke

Zipping up a coat

Sharpening a pencil

Playing an outdoor game

Crossing the road

2. Discuss these ideas in your group.
   - Which do you think would be the most difficult to explain? Why?
   - Which do you think would be the easiest to explain? Why?

3. Choose two of the ideas and write a short set of instructions for each one. Think about:
   - how to start
   - how to explain everything clearly, so that a younger child will understand it
   - how much detail you need to include
   - getting points in the correct order
   - using diagrams and pictures.

Explanatory texts

Reading and understanding an explanation

1. Read this explanation of how our teeth work.

   Taking a bite

   The process of digestion begins in the mouth. Teeth break up the food and grind it into smaller pieces. Only the lower jaw can move, so the lower teeth work against the upper teeth to bite and chew. Teeth have to be hard and tough to do this job. They are covered with a layer of enamel – the hardest substance in the body.

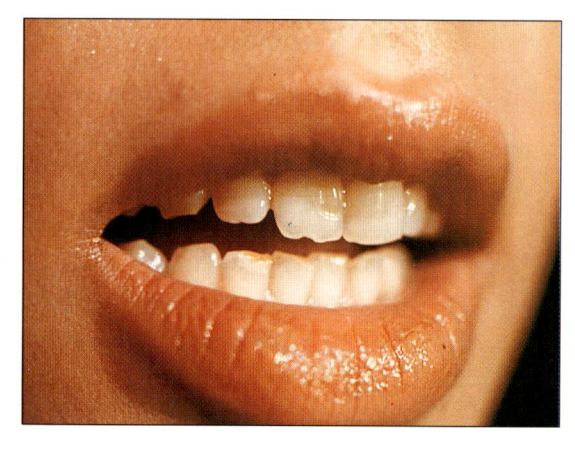

   Teeth are like precision tools – shaped to do different jobs. You use the incisors, the eight flat, sharp front teeth, to take a bite or slice of food. The four long canines, fang-like teeth on each side of the front teeth, are good for gripping and tearing. The eight premolars tear and grind the food, and twelve large flat molars at the back of your mouth grind the food down into small pieces. Adults have 32 teeth altogether.

   Angela Royston
   Eating and Digestion

2. Rewrite these sentences in the passive.
   - Teeth break up the food and grind it into smaller pieces.
   - You use the incisors to take a bite.
   - The eight premolars tear and grind the food.

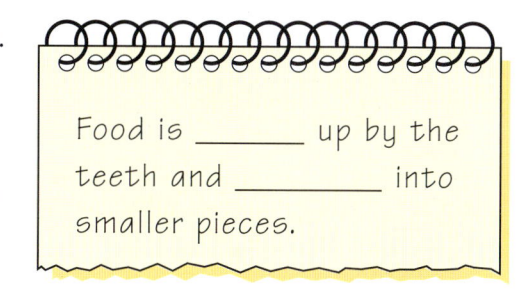

   Food is _____ up by the teeth and _____ into smaller pieces.

3. Four different kinds of teeth are mentioned in the second paragraph. Name them and the special jobs they do.

4. Explain in your own words:
   - in what way teeth are like 'precision tools'
   - in what ways canines are like 'fangs'.

5. Discuss this explanation with the rest of your group. Is it as clear as possible? How could it be improved?

89

Reports

Evaluating a written report

1. Read this report about animal homes.

Animal homes

Big animals like whales have no homes. Neither do animals with hooves like horses and musk oxen. But tiny animals such as mice need somewhere safe to sleep and hide from their enemies. Creatures as small as wrens and as large as bears have nests or dens where they can bring up their young.

Some animals find their homes ready-made. Hares rest in a form. This is just a dip in the ground. Bats sleep in caves or hollow trees, and a hollow branch is a home for a racoon.

Other animals make homes where they can shelter. Most have no hands like ours to help them, so they use whatever tools they have such as beaks, teeth and claws.

Harvest mice weave dry grasses into a hollow ball. Potter wasps mould mud into a pot-shaped nest. Weaver ants pull leaves together and glue them into a kind of silk. Foam-nesting tree frogs use their legs to beat jelly into a foam that keeps their eggs and tadpoles moist.

Weaver ants at work   *Weaver ants' leaf nest*

Rabbits and moles use their paws to dig long tunnels. Moles live underground all the time. Rabbits sleep, breed and hide in burrows. Only slender enemies like stoats can chase a rabbit down its hole. Even then, a rabbit may escape from its burrow by another entrance.

D. Lambert
First Picture Book of Animals

2. What do you think is the purpose of this piece of writing?

3. How is the information organised?
    - Write a note to label the main idea in each paragraph.
    - Is it easy to do this? Explain you answer.

4. Do you think this report is clearly organised?
    - Write a short explanation, giving reasons for your opinion.
    - If you do not think it is well organised, suggest ways of improving it.

A group of rabbits near a burrow

Bats sleeping in a cave

Persuasive writing

Evaluating a leaflet

1. Look closely at this leaflet that was pushed through someone's letterbox.

SAVE OUR SCHOOL
ST PAUL'S VILLAGE SCHOOL
STOP THE CLOSURE!
Public Meeting – Town Hall, 24 March, 7pm

The local council wants to close down our village school. For the sake of our children's futures, we **MUST stop them!**

St Paul's School opened in our village in 1876. It has survived two World Wars and countless generations of children. The quality of education provided by the superb staff is absolutely outstanding. Now some petty council officers want to save a few pounds from their budget by destroying all this good work. **WE SAY NO!**

Are we expected to believe that closing our school will really help to save the council money? The real truth is that the council just can't be bothered to deal with our delightful little school. Surely they can see that closing the school will do them no good? **WE SAY NO!**

What will future generations do if the school closes? We believe that without the school, young families will move away from the village, and our lovely community will soon die. We must stop the closure! **WE SAY NO!**

STOP THE CLOSURE – STOP THE TEARS!

Can you help? Call the Campaign Manager – Veronica Smithson – on 01511 134765

---

2. Do you think that this is an effective leaflet? Why? Give two reasons.

3. Write three examples of persuasive devices used in this leaflet.
    - Explain what each example aims to do.
    - Does each example work well? Give reasons.

4. How could the leaflet be improved?

Improvements
The text could be cut down to make it easier to read.

Letters

Reading and evaluating letters

1. Here are the beginnings of four letters.

To the editor of the local newspaper

Dear Editor
I am a retired police officer with 24 years' service in this beautiful town of ours. It breaks my heart to see teenagers running and yelling in the streets on their way home from school ...

To a local councillor

Dear Councillor Jones
The state of the pond in Newbold Park is an absolute disgrace. It makes me very angry when I think how much money I pay in council tax, and you cannot even look after a pond...

To the editor of a wildlife magazine

Dear Editor
I am carrying out a survey into the increasing numbers of magpies in residential areas, and would be grateful if your readers could provide me with the following information:
1) Sightings of magpies in...

To the local newspaper

Dear Gazette
Why oh why oh why must we put up with cars racing through our streets? Surely the time has come to lower the speed limit to at least 20 miles per hour. Research shows that this would considerably reduce the risk of road accidents, and especially fatal and serious injuries to

2. For each letter, write a short note giving your ideas about why the writer wrote the letter and how the letter is written.

3. Choose one of the beginnings. What do you think the writer said next?
   - How do you think she or he said it?
   - Write the next few sentences, using the same writing style.

Letters

Analysing a letter

1. Ten-year-old Nina wrote this letter to her local council.

>
> Parks Department
> Hexford Borough Council
> Hexford HX1 1BD
>
> 12 Brook Street
> Hexford HX6 5FY
> 22 August
>
> Dear Sir or Madam
>
> I would like to thank you for building a new play area in Newbold park. My brother, who is five, and his friends love playing there and it is very safe but lots of fun. Mums and Dads have somewhere to sit as well.
>
> But what about older children like me and my friends? What is there in the park for us to do? The answer is NOTHING. This is just not fair.
>
> You can't blame children of my age and older for getting into trouble when there is nothing for them to do. They all get bored and so of course they look for mischief like running through the flower beds. Children who do this kind of thing always end up getting into more serious trouble.
>
> I think you should build an adventure playground where older children can play. Then they would have somewhere to go and there would be no more trouble. I know this would cost a lot of money, but you would not have to pay to repair any more damage. It makes good sense.
>
> Yours faithfully
> Nina Dauncey

2. What do you think about Nina's point of view in this letter?
   - Does it make good sense?
   - What are the strong points? What are the weak points?

3. Write a detailed report on the letter.
   Think about how Nina:
   - gets the reader's attention
   - exaggerates things
   - uses questions
   - tries to get the reader on her side.

95

Letters

Writing a letter

1. Read this letter, another one that Leigh wrote to Mr Henshaw.

Tuesday, 9 January

Dear Mr Pretend Henshaw,

My little cheesecake was missing at lunchtime which made me mad. I guess somebody noticed Joe Kelly's lunch was really mine. When I went to throw my lunch bag in the garbage, Mr Fridley said, "Cheer up, Leigh, or you'll trip over your lower lip."

I said, "How would you feel if somebody was always stealing the good stuff from your lunch?"

He said, "What you need is a burglar alarm."

A burglar alarm on a lunchbag. I had to laugh at that, but I still wanted my cheesecake.

Dad should be phoning any day now. When I said that at supper (chilli out of a can), Mom said for me not to get my hopes up, but I know Dad will remember this time. Mom never really says much about Dad, and when I ask why she divorced him, all she says is, "It takes two people to get a divorce." I guess she means the same way it takes two people to have a fight.

Tomorrow, I am going to wrap up my lunchbag in a lot of Scotch tape so nobody can sneak anything out of it.

Beverley Cleary
Dear Mr Henshaw

2. What do you think has been happening?

3. What are Leigh's two main worries? What are his thoughts and feelings about each of them? Make some notes.

4. Now imagine that it is Wednesday, 10 January.
   - Imagine that things happen to change the way Leigh thinks about both of his worries.
   - Decide what these events could be and how Leigh reacts to them.

5. Write the letter that he sends to Mr Henshaw on Thursday, 11 January.